Dear You:

This is a personal movie, sound track out of my own past, 95 true photo images I stopped out of time.

You could make your own paper movie, from that box of snapshots, poems, diaries and old letters. But this one is mine. My hope is you find in it some bread and wine for your own journey.

Come walk with me awhile. We can be friends of the road. We could even be lovers, so intimate that for a brief hour you'll see the world through my eyes.

Lou Stoumen

A Hand Press Book
published by
CELESTIAL ARTS
Millbrae, California

LOU STOUMEN

CAN'T ARGUE WITH SUNRISE

A PAPER MOVIE®

for my daughters

TOBY
TATIANA

First printing September 1975. Manufactured in the United States of America by Celestial Arts, Millbrae, California. Designed by Michael Glen at Hand Press, Los Angeles, California.

Thanks to the Regents, faculty, students and supporting taxpayers of the University of California. An early experimental version of this book was exhibited at UCLA Art Gallery, hung as a walled movie under title *Dream of Islands.*

Library of Congress Cataloging in Publication Data

Stoumen, Louis Clyde
Can't argue with sunrise / a paper movie

"A Hand Press book"
1. Photography, Artistic. 2. Photography, Documentary. 3. Poems. I. Title
TR654.S76 791.43'092'4 75-262
ISBN 0-89087-052-7
ISBN 0-89087-050-9 pbk.

THE SOUND TRACK

ONE
DREAM OF ISLANDS

drunk at noon

WHEN I WAS A BOY

in a Pennsylvania farm town
half a century ago
I dreamed of far green islands.

This large man writing
was that child
and contains him still.
I dreamed of manhood.
I wanted wheels sail wings
the world.

My father was a doctor in Springtown Pa.
He drove his Ford through the cornfields.
He lanced boils
delivered babies
cut out tonsils
told compassionate lies about cancer.
He often got paid in sausages and eggs.

Lizzi the I

It was a marriage of strangers
arranged by wise Aunt Elizabeth.
Name and street number in hand
Sam Stoumen took the Pennsylvania Railroad
to Youngstown Ohio
where Sarah Grobstein lived
and carried her off
to be a country doctor's wife.

Mother gave piano lessons
to neighbor children
helped run the Doctor's Office
cried some
took me to the Philadelphia art museum
when I was six.

My father was a humanitarian.
He did free surgery
for thousands of patients.
He voted straight Democrat
taught brother Bob and me
to be for the Underdog
which he never defined.

After we moved to Bethlehem Pennsylvania
he once set up as a boxing promoter
brought in lightweight champion Benny Leonard.
But the Lehigh Valley Club hired an aging bum
to fight Benny.
Dad's score was debt
and a pair of autographed gloves.

During the depression
we lost our home to the bank
moved to a rented house down the street.

Fourteen million Americans
couldn't find jobs those days.
Chicago cops massacred steel workers
bullets in their backs.

I remember President Hoover's fat face
in the newsreel
telling the people *Be Patient.*
I remember President Roosevelt on the radio
All We Have To Fear Is Fear Itself.

It's the American Way
PRIVATE ENTERPRISE
DEMOCRACY

Those days before the pill
practically none of the young girls would.
There was traffic to the whores
of Reading and Philadelphia.

My old Liberty High School friends
got themselves cars and steady jobs
if they could find them those hard years
while I hit the road.
They married soft eager girls, and ambitious boys
while I lusted after strangers.

But I set foot at last
on five continents
and a hundred islands.

The islands were green.

Each had its own warm breath and heartbeat.

Their names were music.

Tortola! Ceylon! Cuba!

Puerto Rico! Haiti! Jamaica!

Mona! Madagascar! Zanzibar!

I've seen their palm forests

wake in the trade winds

lithe girls shaking out

their tousled morning hair.

I was advance guard then
of the idiot Tourist
bigboned Kodaked
soaking up rum and sunshine and nooky.

There weren't many of us yankee visitors
those days before the war
only a few businessmen lawyers priests soldiers.
Conrad Hilton and the CIA
hadn't discovered America yet.

One Christmas day
out of film
I lay drunk at noon in a cane field
passing the rum bottle with sugar workers
singing *aguinaldos* to welcome the Christ child.

Toma, Luis! Drink!

Made my first movie in Puerto Rico
a documentary on children.

Puerto Rico is a Paradise.
My camera eye found in it also a Hell.

Listen
do you hear the tubercular cough
of the unemployed sugar worker?
the sobbing of the tired pregnant-again mother?

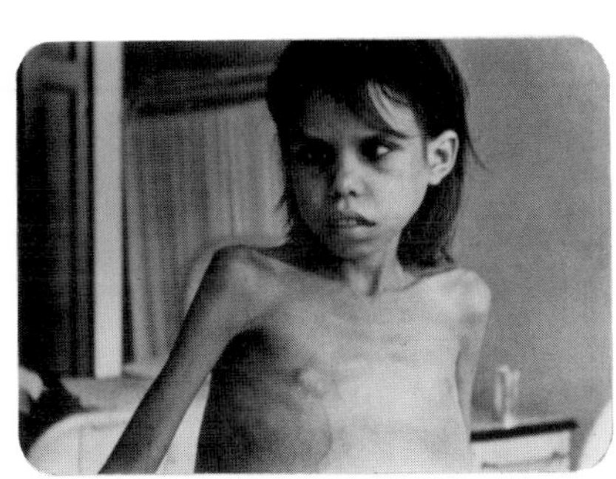
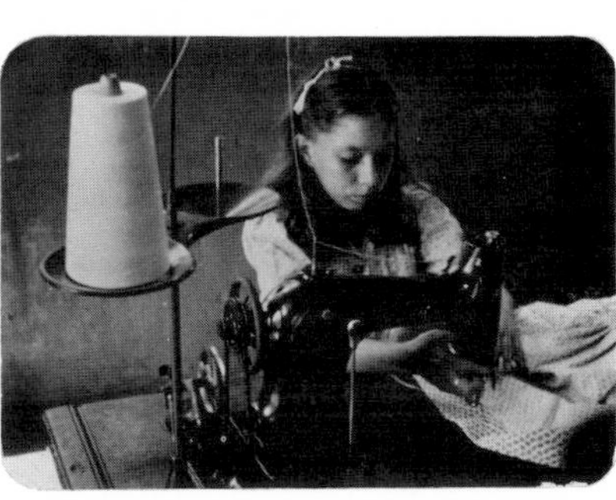
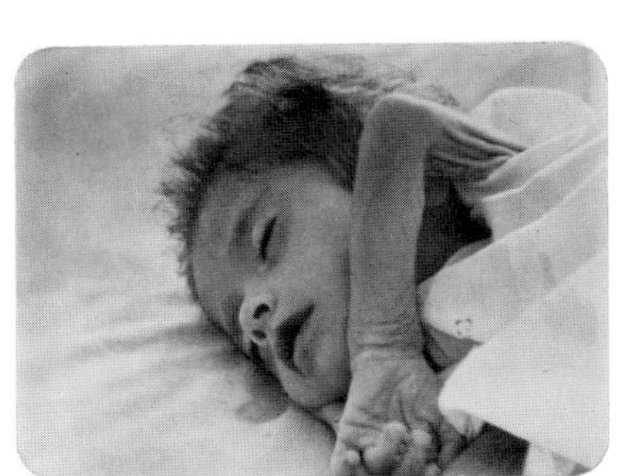

Hello boy. *Que tal?*
I'm glad to meet your eyes.
I think you look crucified
there against the wood of your home
boy Jesus.

I'm sorry about your baby brother.
You found him yes I know
just before this picture was made
fallen from the door stoop
drowned in six inches of muddy water.

My camera eye looked in the face of yaws
malaria filiarisis granuloma.
I dined with lepers on St. Croix.
At a hospital in Santurce
I met a girl sick with amoebic dysentery.
I watched her die.

I lived three years in those islands
a thousand days of green and blue and sungold.
Then I'd enough of lyric beaches
and the people's hunger.
My heart hurt.

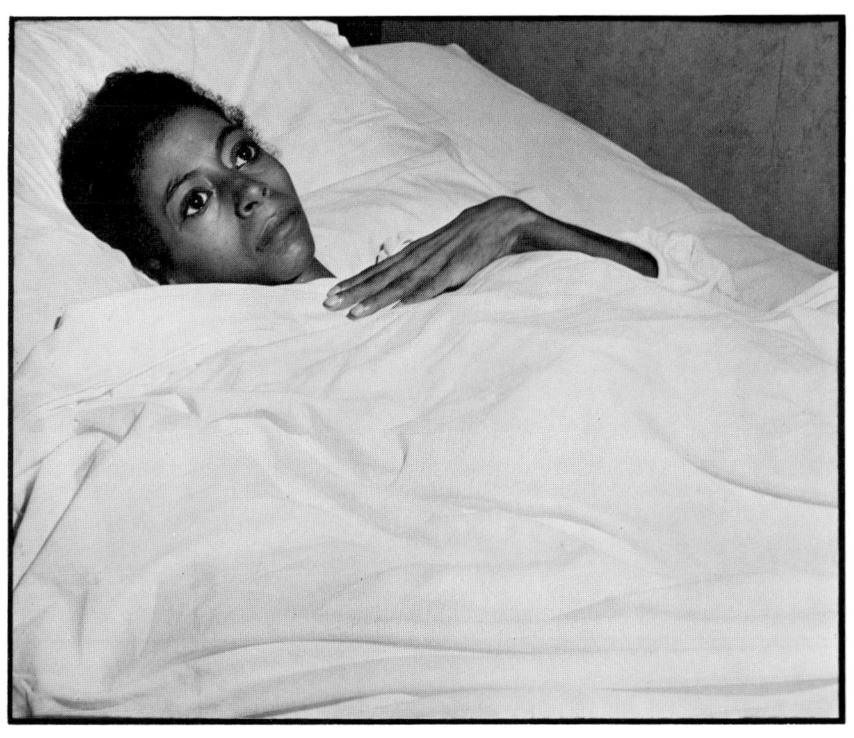

There was one thing more.

Darker.

Older.

You could sense it out in the oldest churches.

In the cane fields it was underfoot.

In the rain forests you could hear sighs.

Each island was in secret mourning.

For its Indians!

They were forest dreamers
those naked brown ones
geniuses of handcraft and fruit
lovers of sea and land.

But their islands were too small for refuge
from the *conquistadores* of Spain
from the French captains the Dutch marines
the English privateers the Yankee slavers
the Danes the Portugese the priests.

Arawak tribe! Carib! Ciboney!
All killed. Some few genes survive
from their raped women.

The sun sets fast in the tropics.
The house of day collapses
like consciousness into sleep.
Life seems shorter.

I thought at last of kin
the clangorous cities of home
the bright brazen girls.
My dream was no longer of islands
but of firm step upon the Continent.

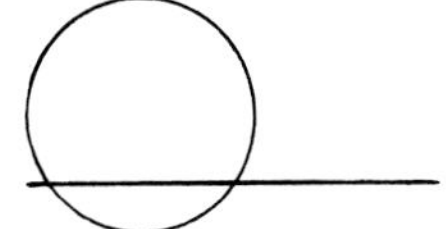

TWO
MEN AT WAR

I'm glad it was Johnny

SOME OF THE BOYS

I went to school with
got their first look at an island
through a screen of fire and fear.

They found no music
in names like Guadalcanal Tarawa Kwajalein.
Their islands were green and soon red
palmsambushed beachesmined.

That's professor of English Gene Sloane center
myself on right. My camera
had a delayed shutter release
so I could get in too.

I was an objector to killing
but didn't want to go to jail.
Besides that was a better war
than the ones we've been having lately.
I went along like everybody
following orders and it wasn't bad.
They made me correspondent
for the army magazine.

When we docked at Kirachi India
I gave away my rifle.
I told myself I would be
God's spy
among the soldiers.
This is my report from that mission.

I fell in with a company of transport airmen in Assam.
From 500 feet over Burma
we parachuted K-rations atabrine ammo
to General Stilwell's malarial footsloggers.

Mostly it rained.
Food clothing paper turned moldy.
Fungus grew overnight on lenses
blistered underarm and in crotch.
Scorpions hid in our shoes.

One night we landed our C47
on a tiny jungle strip behind Japanese lines
snatched out 28 Gurkha and English wounded
vines on a wingtip.

I flew up the Brahmaputra River
waterdragon flashing in the sun.

Our twoengined plane
labored elephantheavy in the sky
burdened with men and gasoline
crates of bombs and whisky.
We wheezed up to 19,000 feet trying for 21
passing oxygenbottles like hashpipes
dodging through the valley passes of Tibet.

The pilot showed us Everest.
Thunderhead clouds he said
were columns of uprushing hurricane
able to tear off our wings.
We landed in China.

I flew on the first B29 raid against Japan.
The American superbomber
was secret till that day
a silver invented bird
of mythic range and fierceness.
It had pressurized lungs
automatic claws and beak
a radar eye.

In phalanx of sixty wings
we thundered out of Szechuan
in the amber light of afternoon
crossed China and the Yellow Sea
and came by night over the steel mills of Kyushu.

26298

Searchlights fingered the dark to touch us. Shellbursts rocked our flight. Most of us laid frightful eggs and got away. We had no concern for civilian steelworkers under our bombs their homes wives babies. Our thought was to keepformation bombaccurately saveourasses.

Kyushu was the most distant bombing target in history.
Later when Pacific islands were conquered
B29s sortied from them
on shorter missions
to Okinawa
Tokyo
Hiro
shi
m
a.

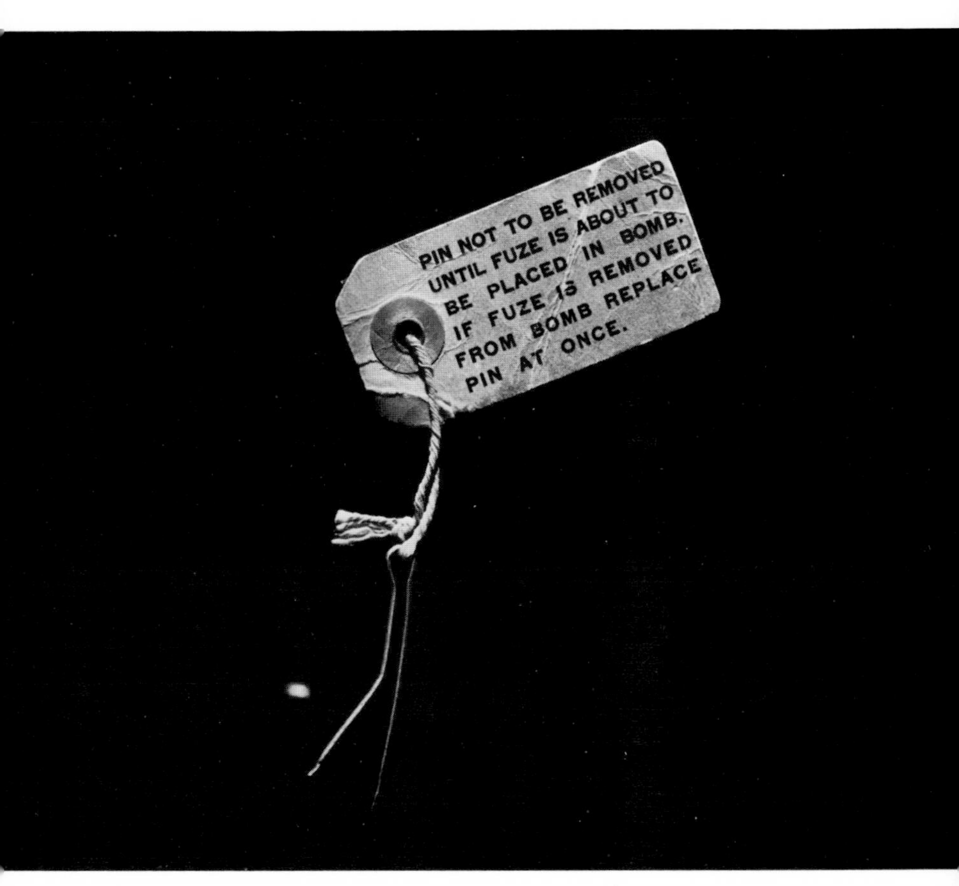
PIN NOT TO BE REMOVED
UNTIL FUZE IS ABOUT TO
BE PLACED IN BOMB.
IF FUZE IS REMOVED
FROM BOMB REPLACE
PIN AT ONCE.

Killing is easier in air.

You never have to fuck a bayonet into a man's belly.

You're only under fire yourself a few minutes.

Air war is technical beautiful.

You watch your enemy arc down in flames

like in the movies.

You watch your bombs walk

with giant flowering steps across a city.

It's only to witness killing

not to do it.

If you get back

you're sure of hotfood cleanbed beer.

There are girls in town.

Maybe friend you were too young or old for Korea.
Maybe Vietnam found you safely in school or jail
or exile or the matrimonial sack.
Want to know how war is?

There's fighting and fear and death.
Mostly it isn't that at all.

For every man in battle
there have to be a hundred driving trucks
cooking saluting telephoning whoring teaching
armingaircraft fixingsubmarines gettingdrunk
washing glassware in the officers mess
inspecting your genitals for VD
writingandreadingandpublishing techmanuals travelorders
inventories requisitions promotions courtmartials
intelligencereports payrolls and regretstonextofkin.

Right private? Heyouthere on the double!

The real enemy is boredom.
Ask any veteran.

The months amputated off your life become years.
You live in a molasses river
of waste incompetence and drunken officers.

The stateside showgirl grinds her rump
at a thousand horny enlisted men
but only services the colonel.

The patriotic leering jokes
of the visiting millionaire asshole comedian
aren't funny.

It doesn't help many
to hear the fat priest from home
bless the murdering at Christmas.

Some of us never had it so good.
Maybe home was a wornout farm
a trap of a job
an unloved wife.
Maybe home was still your father's house.
Maybe home was no work no father
toilet in the hall stopped up.

For us the uniform meant adventure
pride. War was horizon
manhood. Screw those dirty thieving gooks
can't even talk English.

All the war cities of the world

have whorehouses.

BLACK
CAT
BLACK
CAT

Yes sir we sure were drunk. Stanley
was drunkest of all sir. He couldn't walk
he was unconscious in a bedroom so two of us
took his arms and legs to carry him back to the ship.
Well sir we come to this tattoowallah and

Well sir yes sir it was my idea. Anyway
the needle woke Stanley up he didn't object
he enjoyed it he just wanted to know
what the tattoo was going to be so

Sir we told him it was an anchor and a rose.

But sir soon's it was done we showed him a mirror.
and sir he laughed we all laughed
hysterical so we couldn't breathe. Stanley
was laughing most pounding his foot on the floor
laughing to bust his ass. So I don't see sir
why he's bringing charges against us now.

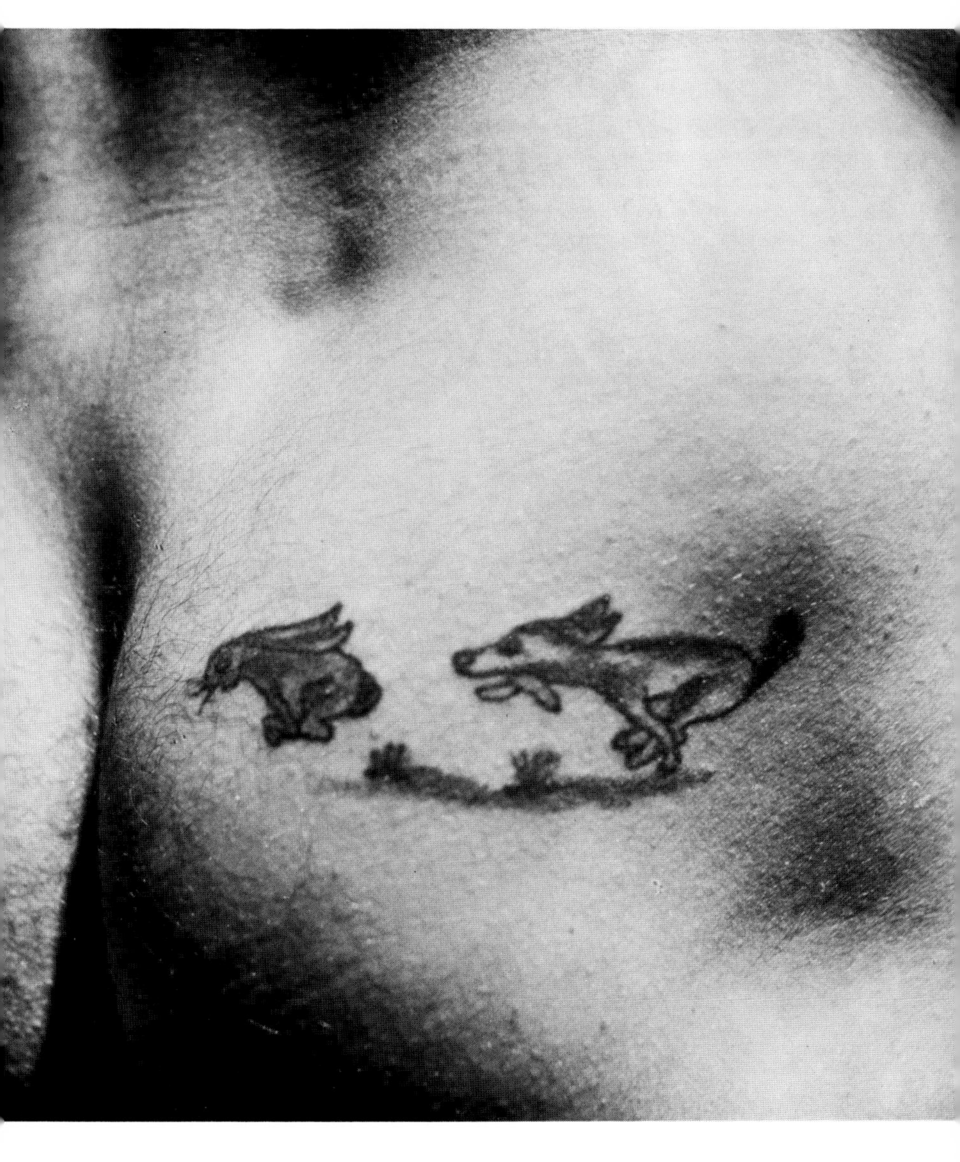

One afternoon in Calcutta
I called the first meeting of the United Nations.
In the doorway of a bar.
Have a drink buddy?

We were a Security Council in our cups
the New Zealander the Sikh the Aussie
the Chinese the two Englishmen the Maharati
the Pathan the West African the Rajput
and we four Americans. Guess who's which.

We never got to declare peace.
We couldn't figure a way
behind our officers' backs
to invite the Japanese and German enemy.

More than fifty million men women children

died in that war.

Should a man kill?

Should an invaded nation resist?

What is a nation? South Vietnam? Cuba? Israel? Taiwan? Spain?

Czechoslovakia? The Confederate States of America?

Do the means determine the end?

Am I my keeper's brother?

It's bitter truth
that the closest a lot of my generation ever got
to loving
was in the murderous comradeship of battle.

Sweet wife
do you think you can ever love your husband
half so much
as his tailgunner did after fifty missions?

See the pretty palms shredded by artillery?
See the brave soldiers advancing inland on the island?
This photo was made on Eniwetock by Sgt John Bushemi
just before he got his throat cut by a mortar fragment.

Johnny was a beautiful photographer in my outfit.
On the hospital ship offshore his last gargled words
Make Sure the Pictures Get Back to the Office.

I think about Johnny sometimes
and I put this picture of Johnny's
in my book as a memorial.
Here lies Johnny Bushemi. He was 26.

If I die tomorrow I'll still have thirty years
of breathing laughing working balling Johnny never knew.

I'm glad it was Johnny not me.

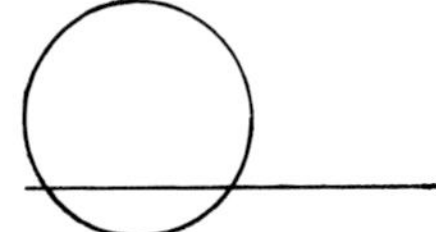

THREE
ASIA

the people's river of sweat

TO WHATEVER FAR LAND A MAN WANDERS

it is in search of himself.

I felt I'd been in Asia before

in that brown hooded face

in that tea house by the river

there that cripple crabbing down the street

there soft in the incense arbor of that silken lady.

Asia seemed returning home
father's house
after a journey of centuries.

Had I never been here before?
Not in Persia? Judea? Hindusthan? Cathay?

The little mother
squatting on the dirt floor of her kitchen
regards my camera eye
across a chasm four thousand years wide.

Here barbaric Christs
still curse the moneychangers
and praise Light.

Here Sound reverberates down the centuries
heartbeat of drums
kissed pipes of Krishna
and Neanderthal.

Girls from Solomon's bed
dance over grass
their scented limbs running deer
their lips honey.

Here too are exploitation madness murder
jungle home of tiger cobra hyena crocodile
and man.
Here is land ancient as death
wise as the night smile of a young wife.

I make pilgrimage to the Taj Mahal
a pearl in sand.
Deep in the underground crypt
an old Sikh sells me
flowerpetals
to dapple on the jeweled sarcophagi
of Mumtaz Mahal and her King.

Among Asia's thousand gods
the most fanatically worshipped is
Hunger.

Cannibalism is done in His name
and child selling
and murder
and the eating of earth.

Hunger's holy word is *Baksheesh! Alms!*
His alter the burning ghat
His angels the carrionhawk and the vulture
His stigmata a marketable deformity.

Sahib! Baksheesh!

You want jolly-jolly Sahib?

You no want me I take you my seestaire

she thirteen very clean Sahib

virgin girl from country.

You give me seegarette Sahib?

All Asia is work muscle survival.
Greater than the Ganges and the Han
is the people's river of sweat.

Peasant families calfdeep in paddy mud
from dawn till dusk
pickers of tea in the steaming fields
weavers of cloth and of straw
watercarriers hunters healers fishers tanners
miners smiths woodcutters pimps whores dacoits
collectors of taxes and of dung
ant armies of coolies crucified between cart shafts.

I was a wanderer in Asia
a long generation ago.

I was young then
a foreign soldier bringing war.
What I remember now
an age and a globe away
is not war
but the people the friends
working worshipping cheated dying studyingrevolution
flowering with children.

I remember the walled city of Chengtu
green rain in the bamboo groves of Sylhet
a hooded family of three lurching camelback
over the Sind desert.
I remember carp and children
in the pools of Intally
and how monsoon mornings the mist
rose golden to the sun.

I remember the smell of carbidelamps
mulberrywine and women
in gay Kweilin.
I still hear the laughter of a hundred cities
the street cries
the shouts of love and commerce and anger.

How could I forget the tender maid of Calcutta
Sunnanda the flowerfresh
and her mother who sang with Tagore
her father who marched with Gandhi?
How could I forget love
and grief
for the gentle professor of Kunming?
He served us tea in jade cups
was assassinated on campus
by political police of Chiang Kai Shek
using American weapons.

Sleep well Honored Teacher
young winds freshen in the world.

Hello! Farewell! Auf wiedersehen! Sayonara!
Bon Voyage! Hasta Luego! Nasdarovya!
Habu hao!

The villagers of Szechuan
have never seen a Long Nose so close.
They are delighted how big and foolish I am.
They think the American jeep is very beautiful.
Is it true there are also poor in America?

One immortal family
under the single roof of sky.

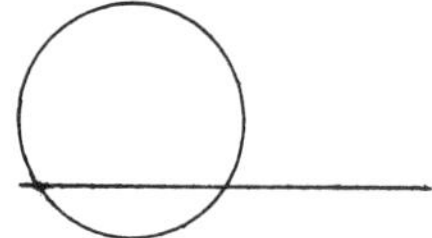

FOUR
U.S.A.

toss her cloudy hair across the continent

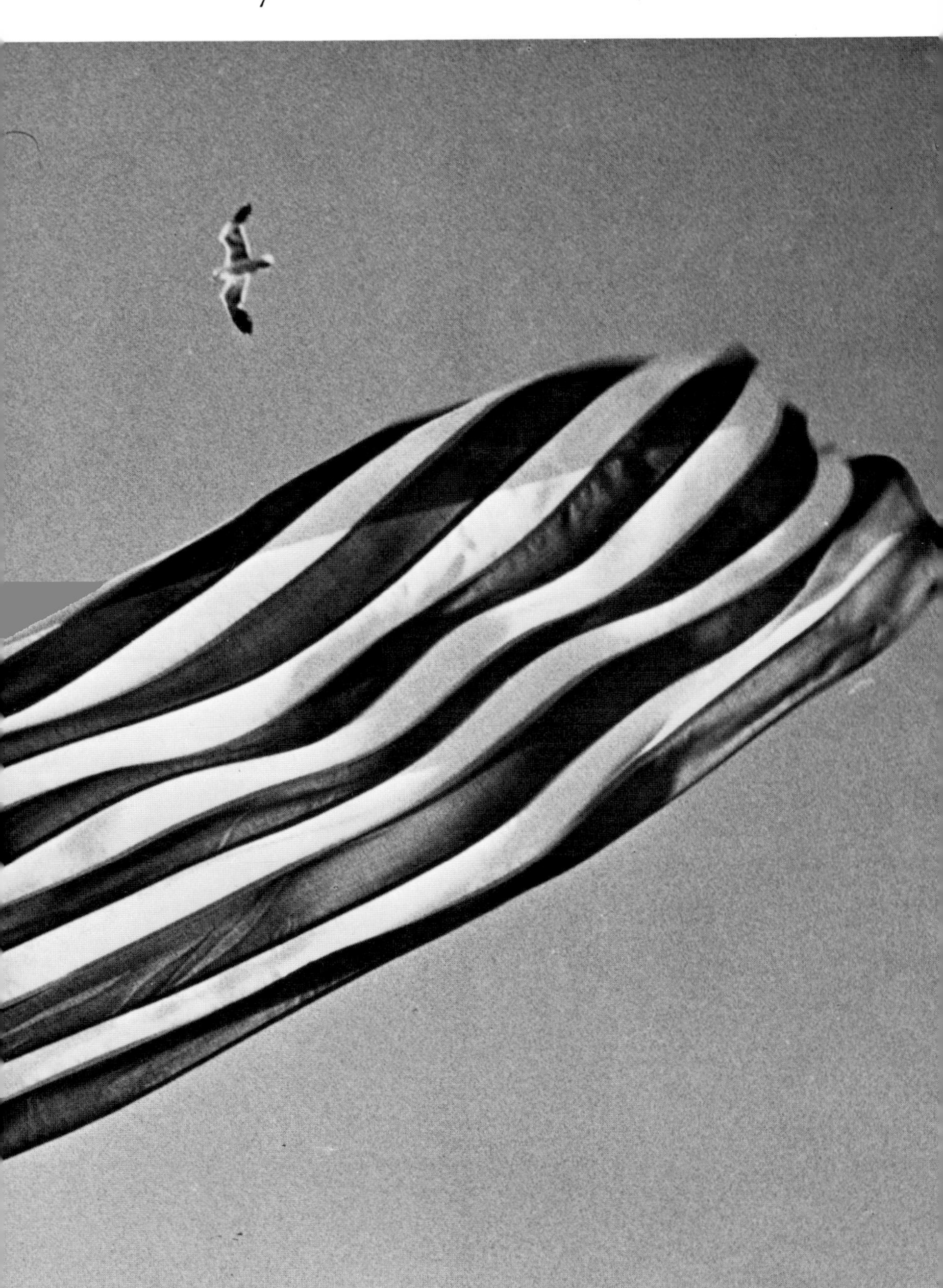

TO WHATEVER FAR PLACE A MAN WANDERS

he must at last come home.

How can you know the world

if you don't know your native land?

How can you know anything

if you don't know yourself?

Camels
CAPITOL
FOUR ROSES
COLUMBIA PICTURES
CHEVROLET
PLANTERS PEANUTS
CHEVROLET
Coca-Cola
BONDS

I've always wondered what makes us Americans.

Is it the beauty of our land
and our love for it
that make an American?

Is it knowing America in its seasons
Spring on the seacliffs of Big Sur
Colorado at roundup time
the green of Mississippi in July
white roll of Pennsylvania hills in winter?

Is it having worked in America
cleared the land of stumps and Indians?
Is it having quilted a bedspread
minedcoal taughtschool organizedaunion
foughtawar builtautomobiles ginnedcotton
enforcedlaw bakedmincepie dreamedarockettothemoon?

Is it farming wheat out of the land
corn berries melons maplesyrup grapes?

10¢
10

Is being an American
singing the songs of America
worksongs Indiansongs seachanties
hymns hillbilly wobbly dixie yankeedoodle
blues acidrock rockofages soul and
willyoulovemeindecemberasyoudoinmay?

Is being an American
knowing about TomPaine TomSwift TomEdison
JoeHill AbeLincoln MaeWest DWGriffith FrederickDouglas
MalcolmX WaltWhitman CalCoolige MargaretSanger
MarilynMonroe CharlieManson RichardNixon?

Is it GOP DAR KKK FBI IRS CBS ACLU CIA
ITT NAACP AFLCIO LSD IOU?

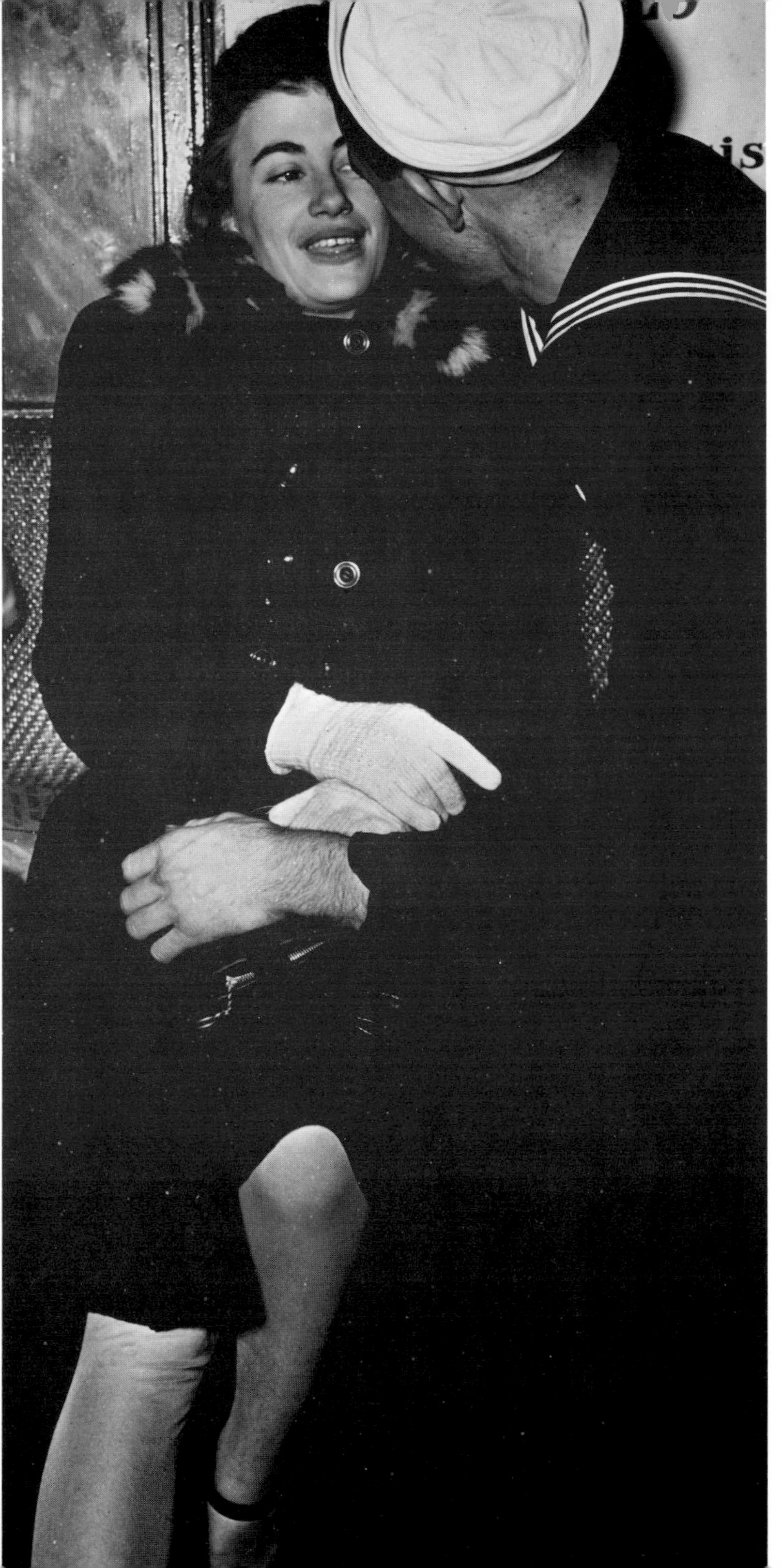

Maybe American life has a trick
of shaping anyone who lives it
giving them an American look
making them be
Americans?

The real trick
is to become a woman a man.
That's hard with all the changes happening.

American life

when I came home from the war

was foodrationing carpools highwages

prettywidows newbabies

businessmen who'd stayed home and got fat.

Hey sailor lemebuyadrink!

You found you weren't dead hooray.

The goldplated discharge button

and a dime

got you a nickel cup of coffee.

Your friends were in London

or lost at sea.

Your girl was married.

No we don't have any openings today

for machinegunners.

WRIGLEY'S
SPEARMINT

Everybody was asking questions.

Under what pile of papers did I mislay my youth?

How did I of all people miss out on the gravy?

Did we have to drop that bomb on Hiroshima?

Why don't you niggers learn professions

and clean up your neighborhoods?

Are you now or have you ever been?

When will the repairman bring back my TV?

Why must man pass so quickly from childhood

to adultery?

AMELS
THE SALVATION ARMY
TIMES SQUARE CORPS
216 W. 48 ST.
WED. SAT. SUN.
8 P.M.
COME
AND
SEE
JOY OF THE LORD SHALL BE YOUR STRENGTH

I looked for my own grief
and found it
moving fast in and out of five cities
many jobs and two marriages.

One day after the war
I came close to numb anxious crazy.
I know what that's about now
can see it in others.
It's loneliness lovelessness.
Crazy equals bodychemistry reading of zero love.
Emptysville.
Shit City.

Only thing I could think to do
was drag a chair to the back porch
put a mirror on it
and shoot myself.

There I was in the mirror
hello upsidedown on the ground glass.
I recognized the man.
My movements were habitual.
I cocked the camera shutter
fired.

Up was only way I could go after that.
All I knew was writing and the camera.
I worked hard was lucky.

There were two Academy Awards on television.
I got a standing ovation at Venice film festival.
I drank brandy with Winston Churchill
smoked his cigar.
I walked and talked in two cities with Aldous Huxley.
I bought a Jaguar automobile with redleather upholstery
raced it from London to Rome.
Marlene Dietrich cooked me an omlette
alone in her Park Avenue apartment
at 3 AM.

Then I dropped out of the movie business
wasn't sure why.

I'd finished a marriage and a movie
in New York City
both to bad reviews
maybe that was it.
Maybe worrying about actors critics productionmoney
I felt I was losing my art.
Maybe without a wife
I wanted to be useful to somebody.

It seemed time again to see a desert
walk under redwoods
shed possessions.
I crossed the country to California
found a job as professor.

Teaching wasn't as I first feared
a copout from struggle.
The students were more engaged
than my boughtoff contemporaries.
They taught me more than I taught them.

This was the tribe
that forced the stopping of a mean war.
They invented new music poetry dress
ethics love.

I trembled before the bloom of the girls
the lean electric force of the men.
I figured some of their dew roses vinegar
might rub off on me.

Hey
could I defect from my generation?

What the young hated most
was lies was war
and got clubbed for it.

Meanwhile we gave medals for high body counts
taught our kids distrust jealousy and winning
killed thousands of ourselves in the streets
including one president.

Sometimes we're so crazy
we think the glory of humans
what we really are
is white is black brown yellow right wrong
communist republican quaker jew presbyterian.

FREE THE
DRAFTEES

But we have all we need
now
in this lovely land
the wheat the circuitry the energysources
the youngpeople the knack.

America could laugh
and toss her cloudy hair across the continent
wash the dried brown
out of the crack of her ass
out of her rivers forests streets air soul.

New cities could be
trees cleanwater and food
care for fish insects animals plants birds children.
People first
corporate profit seventeenth.

In Washington a Department of Joy.
Make truth love and humility
prerequisite for public office.

Let the profiteers
the oilpolluters
the advertising hucksters
the religious liars
the dealers in money and guns
register at last as subversive organizations.

We could do it.
America could help lead humanity through.

There's a worldwide interregnum coming
already here
heavy dues to be paid
for selfishness killing and ecological sin.
But look around us now
at the trees the children the moon.
Hasn't our planet grown suddenly small?

The truth is we're suffering
birthpains!
Humanity is one spirit, mutant.
We flower as irreversibly
as seed to fruit.

1082

Who says we have to flay and scourge ourselves
as our parents did?
Who says a neighbor is rival
or enemy?

The time comes near
to bury nations
in the holy dust of earth
and embrace brothers sisters.

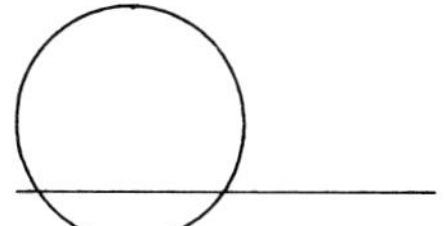

FIVE
THE CHILDREN

can't argue with sunrise

THE VERY YOUNG

know nothing of nations

or wars or islands.

Warm arm holding

is earth.

Mother's breast

is great bowl of sky.

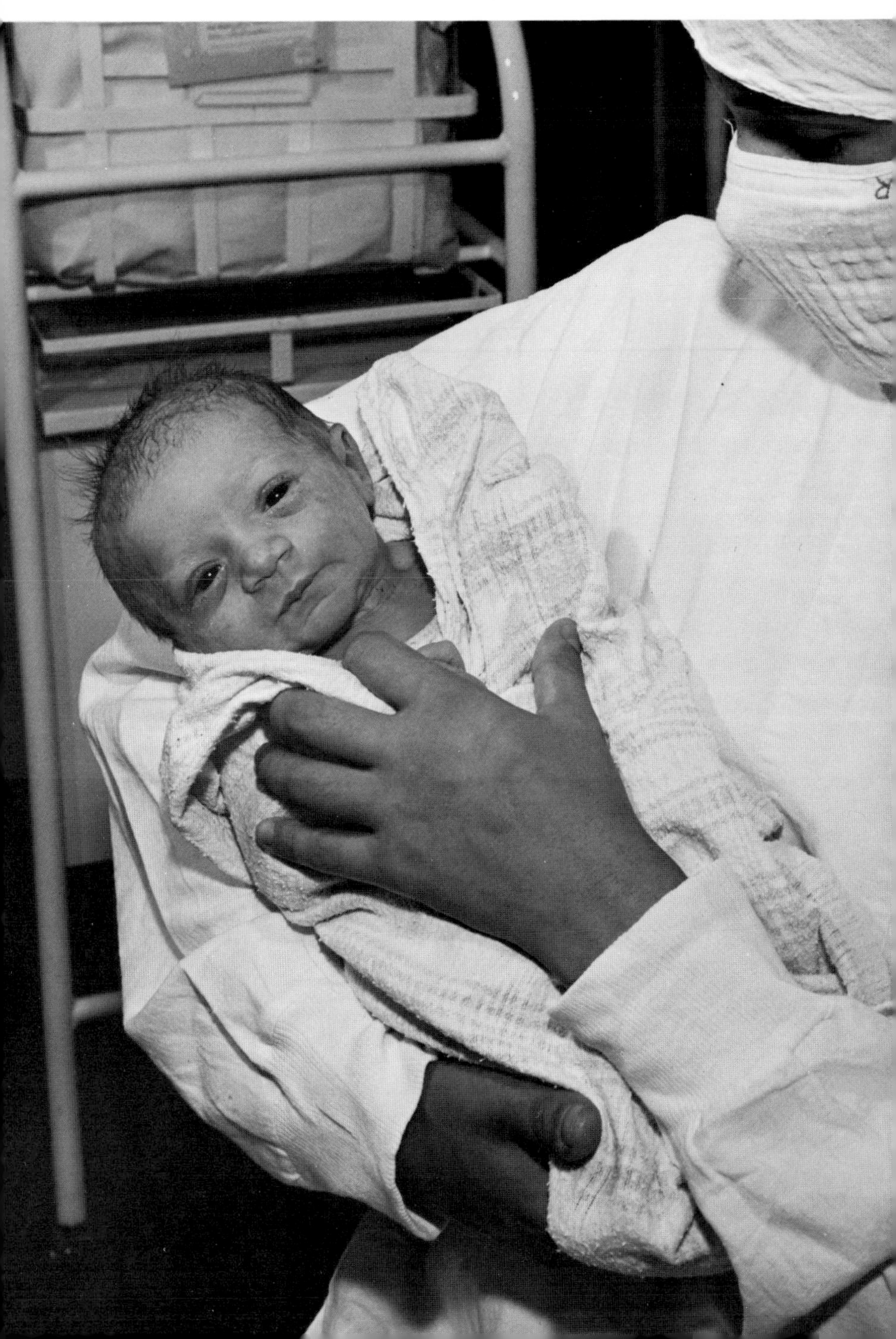

One's own childhood
is the strangest island
so magically far
that once you've left it
you can never return.

Where was I yesterday?
Where was I before I came to this world?

I can't remember how it was
to be a baby.
Did I really come out between mother's thighs?
Did she cry?
Was her pain great?

In all my travels
I looked with wonder at the children.
They seemed old friends
come to greet me
from the distant island of my own beginnings.
There are secrets between us
remembered sharings.

They are sweet of breath and spirit
sacraments on the earth.

As a teacher
I've learned I can teach them nothing
only open a few doors
steady their heads
show them thirty isn't the boneyard.

Oh some of them are a profane crew
heroinaddicts alcoholics hookers groupies
acidpeople godfreaks
warlocks bombers angelsfromhell
and heaven. *Come on baby*
only reason you won't is cause I'm black
right? Or maybe that's why you will?

Begging from tourists in the Haight
on Telegraph on McDougal on the Strip in Boulder.
Hepatitis gonorrhea mononucleosis burglary
syphillis socialism murder freelove *(oh sweetie*
you don't know how free love is
and gentle).

They're troublemakers nasties
tickling in there under mom's bloomers
flashing smiles and nipples at old dad
turning them on
till they know they've missed it all these years.

Busted for grass in the TAC squad sweep
of Venice beach.
Dropping acid in a church of redwoods at Santa Cruz.
Foodstamps and fatherless children.
Greasydishes in the cockroach kitchen.
Beards sandals grannydresses and crablice
hitchhiking to Calvary.

But something's happening on desolation row.
Ain't gwine study war no more.
She's touched your perfect body with her mind.
Light my fire and we shall overcome.
Om mani padme hum.
Relax and float downstream it is not dying.
You don't know what it is
do you Mr. Jones?

SINGER

But you know baby
you and a few scientists prophets poets crazies
and old ones.
The richdiplomats the paranoidpresidents
the bishops and commissars with hot flashes
the ignoramous jackoff generals
your friendly local unionleaders and bookburners
they're lost
holding what they've got
scared mean dangerous
starting late to understand a little.

McCARTHY

No don't ask your parents what time it is
not Mommy and Daddy.

They don't even know enough
to turn off the smog
give up guns
and look in the mirror.

BROW

Changes coming.

Can't argue with Spring after a long Winter.

Can't argue with sunrise.

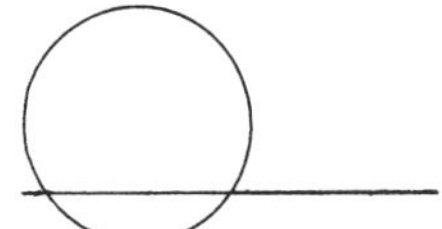

SIX
DREAM OF LOVE

how each eye burns out through air

I DREAM OF ISLANDS

of time

of earth and space

of men and women waking

of love

of the pulsing eternal river of red blood

we all share.

I dream of pubis
male and female
furry island on the body's ocean
birthplace
rebirthplace
mound of resurrection.

I vision the eyes of all the world's people
twin eyelights
skein of netted stars
flashing eyelands
around the ocean orb
of earth.

Do you also dream of eyes?
Do you too in lonliness and sleep
dream of demon lovers
heroic friends?
Do you dream
how each eye burns out through air
to meet and greet
the other's eye
in luminous recognition?

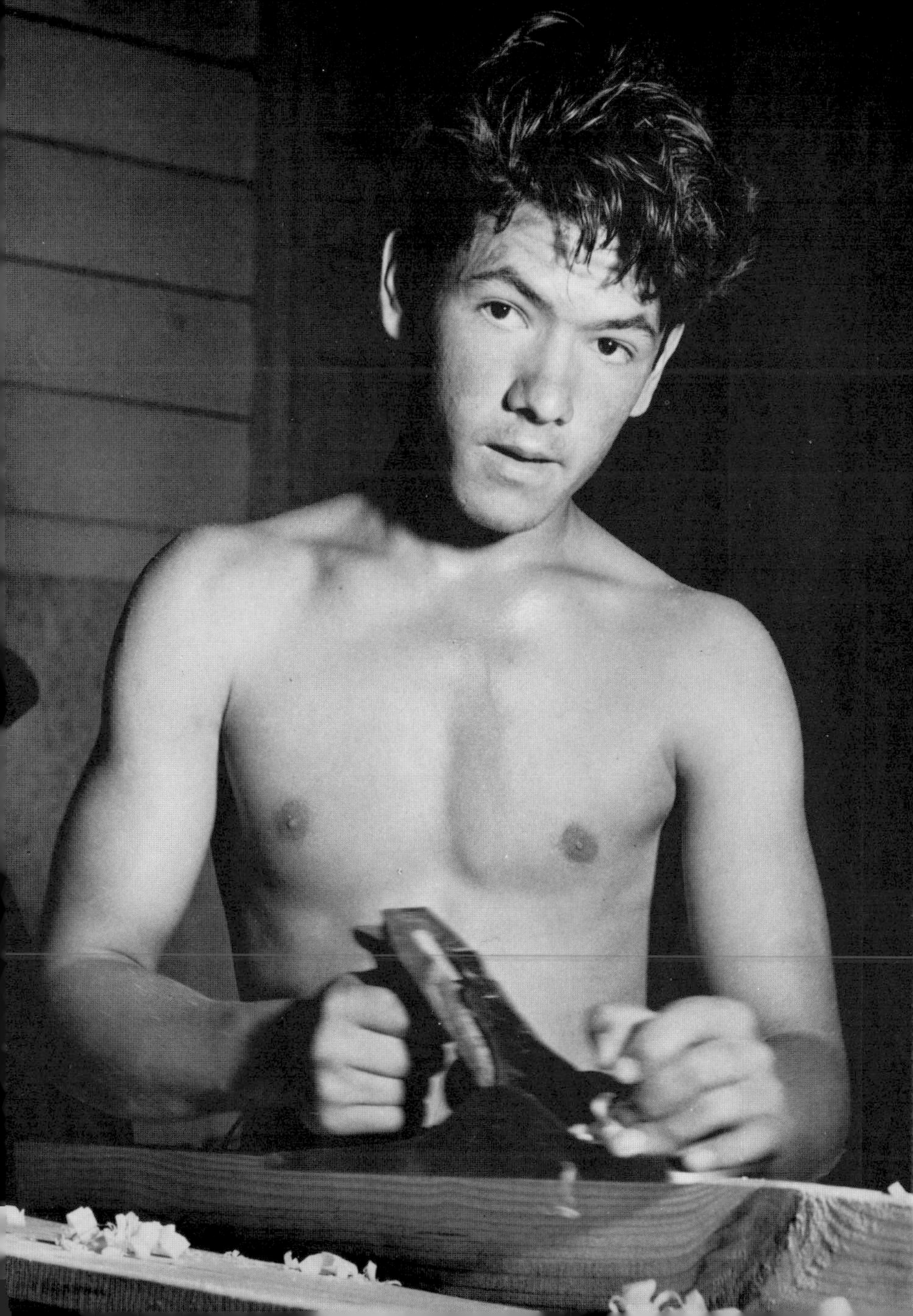

From such visions

the stars of brain's wet cosmos fire

sparking image to memory

light to sense

air to blood

flesh to spirit

island to universe.

When on that beam of light
we two touch
in comradeship or love
our merged spirit
becomes all eye all light.

Can we dream then of a forest
feeling the fall of one leaf?

Can we dream
that a single intake of our breath
involves all the world's air?

Fast then the island brain
empties of our imaged selves
and of the world and memory.

And eyes dim out
and light becomes interior.
Starshine! Sunburst!

We die are born
and I am you in flesh and light
and you are heart and sight to me.
Rainbows flesh across our bones.
We are all divinity.

When I was a boy
in a Pennsylvania farm town
I dreamed of far green islands.
I wanted wheels sail wings
the world.

I'm learning now the true island of dreams
is no distant shore
but the present journey
the work
my being
and yours
ours
this moment
love now if we can make it.

Are you also a lonely traveler?
Are you a fool too?
Aren't you a member of us all?

Do you also look for a flying horse?
A flower that doesn't die?
A kiss from God?

ORIGINAL PRINTS OF PHOTOGRAPHS IN THIS BOOK
can be purchased by writing to the author care of Celestial Arts, 231 Adrian Rd., Millbrae, California.

* * *

An Afterword On Movies Light And Other Mysteries

followed by Captions to the Photographs

WHEN I WAS TEN a friend let me look into the groundglass of his twinlens reflex, and I was hooked. Photographer. Photo grapher. Light artist.

That image in the camera finder had a sudden vital excitement the actual scene (some trees) lacked. The image was more vivid than the "reality." *Wow!* was my thought. *I wanna do this thing.*

What was so special about that image in the camera's finder? Why is the photographic image – especially its galloping multiplier the movie – so very sexy? Answers keep peeling off that question, like skins from an onion.

One early answer is that the camera finder frames a part of reality, separates it from normal 360 degree chaos. The detail becomes significant. We pay attention. And close observation of anything is a meditation, it raises us, makes us feel good.

Another and deeper answer is that photography dusts us with immortality. The camera stops time. Freezes it into formed moments precise as snowflakes. Magic time machine. Microtome. *Zap!* Abraham Lincoln broods. *Zap!* The Wright brothers fly. *Zap(ruder)!* President Kennedy's head explodes. *Zap!* Man walks on moon. *Zap!* There you are, two years old again.

Cartier-Bresson has said his camera search is always for "the decisive moment." That remarkable point in time where movement and meaning converge. An airship blows up. A smile peaks. A child touches a deer's nose. Laura Huxley, on the other hand, has written of "the timeless moment," and photographers like Edward Weston have photographed it. A female nude on sand that is all women. A face, or a tree, that echoes forever.

What makes a *good* photograph? I don't know. There are many styles. Maybe camerawork is an art. One useful test is probably that an excellent photograph *sees* more than the ordinary eye. It opens things up for us, reveals, delights, evokes, disturbs, is, like poetry, a probe to expose truth.

Of course the trouble with photographs is they are singular. They don't move. They have no voice, no music. That's the power of motion pictures. That's how TV killed off *Life* magazine. In my own case, I got bored with the single image. I got seduced by the cinema. You could tell a story in motion pictures. You could *write* a movie. And I was a writer too, loving words. Besides, compared to the special loneliness of the still photographer, making movies is gloriously social. Film-makers get admired, befriended, loved, listened to. There's more money in movies. More power. Film is just maybe (next to music?) the most creatively effective craft/art there is. It combines all the old arts, and some of the sciences. It hits eye and ear and heart. It moves huge audiences. Like music, film is *now*, can be experienced only as process.

For many years, after 1950, I mostly put aside my Rolleiflex and worked in movies, first as cameraman and screenwriter, then as writer-director-producer, then as professor of motion pictures, making an occasional film, a few still photos. Five independent features. Scores of short films and TV things. I made mostly documentaries: *The Naked Eye, The True Story of the Civil War, Black Fox, Image of Love, Winston Churchill–the Valiant Years* (a TV series), *Walt Whitman.*

How can *you* get to make movies? Work. Watch films obsessively. Shoot footage and edit it. Play with sound. Put your attention and time on it. Need to do it more than anything else. Inherit production money, or marry it, or earn it. Go in the back door as bookkeeper, production manager, script girl, actor, film student, wife, lover, son. Go in the front door as writer, film editor, cinematographer, star, stage or TV director, agent, attorney, investor.

Now I find myself working some in still photography again. Close faces. People in the streets. Kids again. Moments of surprise and magic. Prints in my own darkroom coming mysteriously to life out of white paper. There seems to me now in still photography a certain purity, a directness, that I've missed. And in writing poetry, compared to writing screenplay, there is more leanness, more truth, less manipulation of audience, more freedom from the marketplace. Movies are always a frantic enterprise. The technical, financial and personal logistics are ferocious. You spend 95% of your time on contracts, money, casting, technical processes, travel, waiting and cajolery. A film chews a year out of your life.

Making a paper movie can get one as high as any movie-movie. The processes are similar, without most of the time waste and business junk. You combine the flow of cinema with the contemplative intensity of the still photo. The form pleases.

Of course it doesn't have movement. Or sound. Yet the verbal sound track does give a linear flow. The verbal poetry implies, or, indeed, is, sound. When we read "silently," throat and lips and ears do attend. You might even best use this book by reading its sound track aloud. To yourself or to a friend. Work the words a little for their rhythm and emphasis and roll. You be the director, work for a good reading from your self-narrator. And of course you are the movie projector. The little paper machine you hold is hand operated, you turn the pages.

A paper movie is no substitute, is not less than any movie-movie. It's more than a book of poems. More than a collection of photographs. It's an evolved useful form, originated by such as W. Blake, M. Brady, E. Muybridge, A.Ozenfant, A. MacLeish, A. Malraux, Weegee, W. Morris, W. Evans, E. Steichen, P. Strand, A. Adams, E. Smith. Synergism happens. Something alive can be born of the counterpoint between essential words and images.

Marshal McLuhan ("The Medium Is The Message") has suggested that movies are a "hot" medium, since they bombard our senses with rather complete information as to look, color, movement and sound. Radio, McLuhan says, is a "cool" medium, compelling us to create with our own imaginations. Radio makes us work to conjure up the look and movement of personages, events and ideas.

On this McLuhan thermometer the paper movie might seem to register *warm*. For it's hotted-up radio (with illustrations, with instant playback). And it's cooled-down cinema (contemplative; we can stop the flow and meditate on one image). And it's portable, the paper movie. Infinitely repeatable. Inexpensive. Can be shared anytime with friends. And it's a craft, a form, that can be practiced by almost anybody. Let a thousand paper movies bloom . . .

Technical? If you're interested, most of the photographs in this book were made with a 2¼ by 2¼ Rolleiflex. Other cameras used were a 4 by 5 Speed Graphic, a 4 by 5 view camera, a 2¼ by 2¼ Ikonta B, a Graflex and a Foth-Flex. Do I recommend this equipment? Not necessarily. 35mm is big enough for Cartier-Bresson. The massive 8 by 10 view camera was choice of Edward Weston. Polaroid, anyone? 8mm movies? TV tape?

Poetry is essence. Its creation, and its experience, are a kind of love-making – lifting the heart, energizing the body, enlightening the spirit. Photography too is a very high experience, a poetry, a yoga of the eye. I've come only recently to understand one more reason for photography's power. This is perhaps the ultimate reason. One we've always sensed and not often seen. The very inside of the entirely peeled onion. It is that the stuff the photographer works with, his basic material, is not film or camera or paper or movie screen or eye or even "subject matter." The photographer's basic material is the primal stuff of the universe itself: energy/matter, expressed at its highest vibratory rate, in its "thinest" form (particle *and* wave). The photographer's high and holy material is *Light!*

Would this indicate *(gulp!)* that the photographer's task is nothing less than *enlightenment?*

* * *

7 Fishing boats off St. Croix. *Virgin Islands. 1941.*

9 Lou Stoumen, with family friend Minnie Funk. *Photo by Henry Funk. Springtown, Pa. About 1923.*

11 Samuel Stoumen, MD, and Ford. *Springtown, Pa. Photo by Sarah Stoumen. About 1923.*

13 Sarah Stoumen in her wedding dress. *Photo by D. Perel. Youngstown, Ohio. 1916.*

15 Samuel Stoumen, MD. *1950.*

17 Unemployed men. *Houston Street, New York. 1939.*

19 Young couple in car. *Bethlehem, Pa. About 1940.*

21 Palms. *South coast of Puerto Rico. 1941.*

23 Lou Stoumen shooting with Graflex camera. *Puerto Rico. Photo by Narcisso Dobal. 1941.*

25 Eight frame-enlargement stills from L. Stoumen's first movie, "Tropico," made for U.S. National Youth Administration. *Puerto Rico, 1941.*

27 Boy of San Juan slum "El Fanguito" (the Little Mud). *1941.*

29 Dying girl. *Santurce, PR. 1942.*

31 Church. *Plaza of Juncos, PR. 1942.*

33 Woman and crippled boy wait for elevator. *San Juan, 1942.*

79 Girls dance. *Calcutta. 1944.*

81 Taj Mahal from air. *In distance is desert, at right mud flats of Jumna River. 1945.*

83 Beggar. *His disease is elephantiasis. Calcutta. 1944.*

85 Beggar girl. *She sleeps in street. Calcutta. 1943.*

87 Man pulls oxcart. *Calcutta. 1944.*

89 Lou Stoumen and children. *Intally, India. 1943. Photo by George Corbellini.*

91 Woman with baby on back. *Kunming, China. 1944.*

93 Sunnanda Chatterji. *Calcutta. 1944.*

95 Villagers get first close look at an American. *Szechuan province, China. 1944.*

97 Flag on aircraft carrier US Mission Bay. *Off Capetown, South Africa. 1943.*

99 Times Square in rain. *From top of old Times Building. New York. 1940.*

101 American family. *Everybody's gloomy because radio news just said that President Roosevelt was dead. Camden, New Jersey. 1945.*

103 Roundup. *Cowboys drive cattle down mountain to Winter quarters. Near continental divide, Colorado. 1952.*

105 Vegetable market. *Bethlehem, Pa. 1939.*

107 Sailor and girl. *Aboard subway train under New York City. 1940.*

111 Drunken sailors in Times Square. *New York. 1945.*

113 Man and Salvation Army lady. *New York. 1945.*

115 Tenements of Bunker Hill, Los Angeles. *Now replaced by Music Hall development. 1948.*

117 Lou Stoumen in mirror. *Los Angeles. 1949.*

119 Lou Stoumen and Oscar. *Photo by Academy of Motion Picture Arts and Sciences. 1957.*

121 Hannelore Hahn. *Concord, Massachusetts. 1953.*

123 Two students. *University of California, Los Angeles. 1967.*

125 Young war protesters. *Los Angeles, 1969.*

127 American family walks through Washington Square. *New York, 1964(?).*

129 Happy child. *In orphanage. Los Angeles, 1949.*

131 Children in window. *East Los Angeles. 1947.*

133 Children. *Bethlehem, Pa. 1938.*

135 Laughing children. *Occasion is Cinco de Mayo celebration on lawn of public housing development. East Los Angeles. 1950.*

137 Newborn baby. *Queen of Angels hospital. Los Angeles. 1952.*

139 Pensive child. *Venice beach, California. 1953.*

141 Ferryboat boy. *Earns his living poling passengers across river near Chengtu, China. 1944.*

143 Three students in park. *Berkeley, California. 1968(?).*

145 Kiss. *Venice, California. 1971.*

147 Baby, bed, Jesus. *Los Angeles. 1967.*

149 Young black woman sewing. *St. John, Virgin Islands. 1942.*

151 Young family on beach. *Venice, California. 1968.*

153 Couple in park. *Berkeley, California. Around 1969.*

155 Girl with fish. *Nova Scotia, Canada. 1940.*

157 Dawn over South Atlantic off Africa. *1945.*

159 Encounter on beach. *Puerto Rico, 1941.*

161 Figure with long hair. *New York. 1965.*

163 Couple. *St. Louis, Missouri. 1953.*

165 Grandfather and young soldier. *Kunming, China. 1944.*

167 Letitia Innes. *Los Angeles. 1949.*

168 Young carpenter. *Puerto Rico. 1941.*

169 Farm woman, straw hat. *Kunming, China. 1944.*

171 Margaret Maltz. *Los Angeles. About 1949.*

173 Lovers (I). *San Francisco. 1968.*

175 Lovers (II).

177 Lovers (III).

179 Lovers (IV).

181 Lou Stoumen as child (closeup of page 9). *1923.*

183 Lou Stoumen carries movie camera up Lookout Mountain. *Chattanooga, Tennessee. 1953. Photo by Hannelore Hahn.*

185 Walking boy. *Venice, California. About 1971.*